Edmund Goldsmid

The Maner of the Tryumphe of Caleys and Bulleyn

And the Noble Tryumphaunt Coronacyon of Quene Anne, Wyfe unto the

Most Noble kynge Henry VIII

Edmund Goldsmid

The Maner of the Tryumphe of Caleys and Bulleyn
And the Noble Tryumphaunt Coronacyon of Quene Anne, Wyfe unto the Most Noble kynge Henry VIII

ISBN/EAN: 9783337777630

Printed in Europe, USA, Canada, Australia, Japan

Cover: Foto ©ninafisch / pixelio.de

More available books at **www.hansebooks.com**

THE MANER

of the

TRYUMPHE AT CALEYS

AND BULLEYN.

Bibliotheca Curiosa.

THE MANER

OF THE

TRYUMPHE
OF CALEYS AND
BULLEYN,

AND THE

NOBLE TRYUMPHAUNT
CORONACYON OF
QUENE ANNE,

Wyfe unto the Most Noble Kynge Henry VIII.

Printed by WYNKYN DE WORDE, *1532-33.*

Edited by

EDMUND GOLDSMID, F.R.H.S., F.S.A. (Scot.)

PRIVATELY PRINTED, EDINBURGH.
1884.

INTRODUCTION.

———o———

THE two extremely rare tracts here given have been reprinted by Prof. Arber in his "English Garner," if we can call *reprinting* the issuing of a pamphlet not only with the spelling entirely modernised, but also with words and phrases inserted or inverted to suit the Editor's taste. In the "*Tryumphe at Caleys*" Mr Arber has issued the Second Edition, giving us no particulars whatever as to the First. In the list of the noblemen of France, Mr Arber modernises the names and yet gives us a Cardinal *Gramond*, being evidently unaware of the existence of the noble family of de Grammont, and he equally fails to recog-

nise in the Comte de Tonnore, the celebrated Armand, Comte de Tonnerre.
Anne de Montmerancy remains for him
an unknown actor on the brilliant stage,
and yet, surely, the name of the Montmor-
ency must have reached his ears.

I have here given an absolute reprint of
the first edition and have noted at the foot
of each page any variations in the readings
which occur in the second.   Both Editions
were printed by Wynkyn de Worde, probably about November, 1532.   The collation according to the copies in the British
Museum (c. 21, b. 20) is as follows.   It is
a black letter, unpaged tract of four leaves.
Page 1 contains the title, with a woodcut
of Henry VIII. on horseback, with two
attendants.*   Page 2 is blank in the First

---

* I believe the woodcut represents Henry VIII.
although the horsecloth has a *fleur de lys* on it, and not
the Tudor rose ; probably Henry wore the *fleur de lys*
in compliment to Francis.

Edition but contains a list of the noblemen of France in the second. Then come five pages of text in the First Edition, followed by page 8 blank, whilst the Second Edition has six pages of text. The second tract, "The Cornacyon of Quene Anne," was printed by Wynkyn de Worde in 1533. I trust the few notes I have added, either for the purpose of explaining obsolete words or to give a slight clue to the identity of the more important persons mentioned, may prove of use to the student.

EDMUND GOLDSMID.

EDINBURGH, *Nov.* 15*th*, 1884.

The Maner of

the Tryumphe

at Caleys

and Bulleyn.

The Maner

OF THE

𝕿ryumphe of 𝕮aleys and 𝕭ulleyn.*

~~~~~~~~

Cum Priuilegio. †

~~~~~~~~

I ‡ will certyfye you of our newes in the partyes of Caleys.   Fyrst the xj. day of

---

* The title of the Second Edition is as follows :—
The Maner of the
Tryumphe at Caleys and Bulleyn.
The second pryntyge with more addicions as it was done in dede.
Cum Priuilegio Regali,

† In the Museum copy are two MS. Latin lines :
" Congressus lector fuma et fœdera Regum
Et quas vix credas pretiosas perlege pompas."

‡ In the Second Edition, the text begins with :
" The names of the noble men of Fraunce.
Fyrst the frensshe Kynge.[1]

---

[1] *Francis I.*

October whiche was Fryday in the morn-
yng at. v. of the clocke the kynges grace

The kynge of Nauerne.[1]
The Dolphyn Duke of Brytayne Frauncys.
The duke of Orlyaunce Henry.
The duke of Angoulesme Charles.
The duke of. Vendosme Charles.
The duke of Guyse.[2]
The duke of Longouille.[3]
The cardynall of Burbon.
The cardynall of Lorrayne.[4]
The legate and cardynall chaunceler of Fraunce
　　Antony de prayt.[5]
The cardynal tournon.[6]
The cardyna l gramond.[7]
The marques of Lorayne de pont.
The marques of Rochelyne.
The two sonnes of the duke of Uendosme.
The sone of the duke of Guyse conte damualle.[8]

---

[1] *Henry d'Albret, King of Navarre.*
[2] *Claude de Lorraine, first duke of Guise.*
[3] *The duke de Longueville.*
[4] *Jean de Lorraine, brother of the duke de Guise.*
[5] *Antoine Duprat had been tutor to Francis I.　He must have been an old man at this time, for he died in* 1535 *at the age of* 72.
[6] *Of François de Tournon, de Thou says : " Homme d'une prudence, d'une habilete pour les affaires, et d'un amour pour sa patrie, presque au-dessus de tout ce qu'on peut penser."　He died in* 1562.
[7] *Gabriel, Cardinal de Grammont, was the last of the male line of this celebrated family.　His sister married into the family of* AURE, *which then took the name and arms of the de Grammonts.*
[8] *D'Aumale.*

toke his Shyppe called the Swallowe and so came to Caleys by. x. of the clocke.

The conte of saynt Poule Frauncys de Burbon.
The conte of Neuers.
The conute[1] Loys de Neuers conte danseore.
The lorde marshall seigneur de Floraynge.
The lorde myrepois marshall de la foy.[2]
The conte de porsean.
The conte de bresne.
The conte de tonnore.[3]
The conte de sensare.
The conte de grant pre.
The conte d'apremont.
The lorde greate mayster Anne de momerancy.[4]
The lorde admarald Philyp Schabbot.[5]
The lorde grand esquyer Galliot.
The prynce of molse.
The conte de tande.[6]

---

[1] *Sic.*

[2] *A descendant of Guy de Levis, who was elected marshall of the Crusaders who marched against the Albigenses ; hence his successors were all called Marechaux de la Foi. He received the lands of Mirepoix, in Languedoc, in return for his services. The family became very illustrious, and we refer readers who have the time and patience to study a very curious piece of family history, to the writings of Cartier and Lognac.*

[3] *The Comte de Tonnerre.*

[4] *He began life as page to Francis I., became Constable of France in* 1538, *and died at the age of* 74, *at the battle of St Denis, killed, it is said, by a Scotsman named Stuart.*

[5] *Phillippe Chabot, Seigneur de Brion, in Poitou, a great protégé of the celebrated Duchesse d'Etampes.*

[6] *This is undoubtedly Honorat, son of Villars, Comte de*

And there he was receyved with processyon
and with the mayre and the lorde delite

The conte de villars.[1]
The conte de estampes Johan de la berre.[2]
The conte de chambre.[3]
The lorde canamples.
The lorde barbeluiez.
The lorde hummeres.[4]
The lorde roche piot.
The lorde of saynt Andrews.
The lorde montigeu.
The lorde roche guyon.
The lorde piennes.
The lorde pontremy.
Monsieur de longe.
Monsieur de belley.[5]
The archebysshop of Roan.
The archebysshop of Vienne.
The bysshop of Lyseures.
The bysshop of Langres.
The bysshop of Charttres.
The bysshop of Lymoges.
The bysshop of beauuoys.
The bysshop of Auuergne.

---

*Tende, natural son of Philip, duke of Savoy. Villars had
been killed at Pavia in* 1525. *Honorat's daughter married
the great duke de Mayenne.*
 [1] *André de Brancas, comte de Villars.*
 [2] *Jean de Berri, comte d'Etampes.*
 [3] ? *Chambéry.*
 [4] *Probably Henry de Crévant d'Humières, ancestor of
the celebrated marechal d'Humières.*
 [5] *Probably Martin du Bellay, prince d'Yvetot.*

and all the speres* and the sowdyours in araye with a greate peale of gonnes and laye in Caleys tyll the Sondaye seuenyght after. And on the. xvj. day of October my lorde of Norffolke accompanyed with my lord of Darby and a great nombre of gentilmen besydes mette with the great mayster of Fraunce vj. myles fro Calays at ye englysshe pale the sayd great mayster hauynge two greate lordes in his company of theyr ordre and a hondred gentylmen attendynge vpon them. And there my lorde of Norffolke and the greate mayster deuysed the place where the two kynges sholde mete whiche was at Sandyngfelde. And that done they wente bothe to Caleys with theyr companyes. And the sayd greate mayster with dyuerse other straungers dyned that daye with ye Kynge.

The bysshop of Macon.
The bysshop of Castres.
The bysshop of Paris.
The bysshop of Angoulesme.
And as concernynge the nobles and ryall states of this realme it nedeth not to expresse by name.

*Knights.

And after dyner my lorde of Norffolke brought them forth on theyr way a myle or two and so departed for that tyme. And on the mondaye the. xxj. daye of October the Kyng of Englande toke his waye to mete with the frensshe kyng at the place before appoynted with vij. score all in veluet cotes afore hym lordes and Knyghtes and xl. of his garde and other to the nombre (as we thynke) of. vj. hondred horses and as well horsed as euer was seen. And ye Kyng our mayster mette with the frensshe Kyng at Sandyngfelde within the englysshe pale thre myles. There the frensshe kynge taryed for our mayster the space of an houre or two the frensshe kynge beynge accompanyed with the kynge of Nauerne the cardinal of Loreyn the duke of Vandome and * with dyuerse other noblemen well and rychely appoynted beynge of lyke nombre as our kyng was of that is to saye vj. hondred psones. † There was the louyngest met-

---

* The Second Edition omits: " and." † Persons.

yng that euer was seen for the one
embraced ye other v. or vj. tymes on
horsbacke and so dyd the lordes on eyther
party eche to other and so dyd ryde hande
in hande with greate loue the space of a
myle * and than they dyd lyght of theyr
horses and dranke eche to other the
frensshe kyng dranke fyrst to our kyng
and whan they had dronke they embraced
eche other agayne with great loue and so
rode towards Bulleyn our kynge on the
ryght hande. And whan they came
within a myle of Bulleyn there mette
with the kynges the Dolphyn beynge
accompanyed with his two bretherne the
duke of Orliaunce and the count or erle
of Angolame very goodly chyldren and
attendyng vpon them four cardynalles with
a M. horses very well beseen. And whan
they came nere to ye towne the frensshe

---

* The Second Edition inserts: "At ye metyng of these
two noble kynges there were sacres and sacrettes cast
of and at dyuerse flyghtes two kytes were beten
downe which were sooryng in ye ayre w^h such lyke
pastyme whiche greatly pleased al the nobles on bothe
partyes.

2

kynge caused our mayster to tary whyles
ye gonshot was shotte whiche was herd
fro Bulleyn. **xx.** englysshe myles of.
And so entered the towne where stode the
captayn with the sowdyours in good ordre
and aboue them stode a hondred swyt-
sheners of the frensh kynges garde in theyr
dublettes and theyr hosen of yelowe veluet
cutte goodly persons * and aboue them
stode cc. of the frensshe kynges garde
more scottes and frensshmen in cotes of
yelow blewe and crymsyn veluet beryng
halberdes in theyr handes and aboue them
stode cc. gentylmen beyng in theyr gownes
well and rychely beseen euery man hauyng an ax † in theyr handes and theyr
captaines standyng by them. And so they
taryed in Bulleyn mondaye tuysdaye
Wednesday and thursday all daye.‡ And

---

* The Second Edition reads "persons" thus "psones."
† The Second Edition has "a batayle ax."
‡ The Second Edition inserts: "The tuysday beynge
ye seconde day of hys there beyng the frenssh king
gaue our kyng ryche apparayle wrought with nedle
werke pyrled¹ w^h golde in ye whiche lyke apparayle

---

¹ *Fringed.*

for the greate chere that was there no man can expresse it. For the kynges grace was there enterteyned all at the frensshe kynges costes and charges. And euery daye noble men of Fraunce desyred our nobles and gentylmen home to theyr lodg-ynges where as they founde theyr houses rychely hanged greate cupbordes of plate sumptuous fare with syngyng and playenge of all kyndes of musyke. And also there was sent vnto our lodgynges great fare with all maner of wynes for our seruantes and our horsmeet payd for and al at theyr charges. And euery day ye frensshe kyng

bothe ye kynges went to our lady chyrche in Bulleyn And at that time our kyng optayned release and lyberte of the frenssh kyng for all prysoners at that tyme beynge prisoners in Bulleyn. And in lykewyse dyd the frenssh kyng in Caleys of our kyng and mayster at his there beynge and optayned grace for all banysshed men whiche wolde make sute for theyr pardon. And to esteme ye rich trauerses[1] y^t were in Bulleyn at our lady chyrche and in Caleys in our lady chyrche in lykewyse for bothe the kynges the riche ordynaunces and prouysyon for the same it is to moche for to wryte. And as for the greate chere " &c.

---

[1] *Low curtains.*

had at dyner and souper with hym cer·
tayne noble men of Englande. And the
kynges grace had in lykewyse certcyn of
theyr nobles at dyner and souper during
ye tyme of theyr beyng at Bulleyn.
And this contynued with as great chere
and familiarite as myght be. And as con-
cernyng ladyes and gentylwoman there *
was non there. And on frydaye folowynge
the kynges came to Caleys. And the
dolphyn with the cardynalles and all theyr
gentylmen brought the kynges vnto
ye place where they fyrst mette and than
departed. The frensshe king had great
cariage † for there came ccc. mules laden
w^h stuffe. And ‡ whan they came to

---

* The Second Edition omits: "there."

† Baggage.

‡ The Second Edition reads for: "And when they
came to Calais" . . "And so commynge towarde
Caleys the duke of Rychemonde accompanyed with
bysshops and many other noble men that were not with
the kyng at Bulleyn and all the kynges garde which were
with all other meruaylously well horsed and trymde
they stode in aplace appoynted in aray and good order
in the way two mile out of Caleys where the frensshe
kynge sholde come who saluted ye frensshe kynge with
great honour in lyke maner as the kynge our mayster

Caleys they were saluted with great melody what with gonnes and all other instrumentes and the ordre of the towne it was a heuenly syght for the tyme First at Newnam bridge. iiij. c. shotte at the blockhous. xl. shot at Rycebanke toure. iij. c. shot within y^c towne of Caleys. ij. m. shot great and small besydes the shyppes it was all nombered. iij. m. shot. And at Bulleyn by estymation it past not. cc. shot but they were great peces. Also for the ordre of the towne there was set all seruynge men on the one syde in tawny cotes and sowdyours on the other syde all in cotes of reed and blewe with halberdes in theyr handes. And so the kynges came ryding in the myddes and so the frensshe kynge went to staple hall which is a pryncely hous and vpon saterday bothe the kynges rode to our lady chyrche to masse. And at after noone* bothe theyr counselles

---

was saluted at Bulleyn with amykable and moost goodly salutacyons as euer was seen they were saluted w^h great melody," &c. &c.

* For "after noone" the Second Edition reads, "after onne."

sate togyder. And vpon sondaye both
ye kynges herde masse in theyr lodgynges.
And at after-noone the kynge of Englande
went to Staple hall to the frensshe kynge
and there was bothe bere baytynge and
bulbayting tyll nyght. And at nyght the
frensshe kynge souped with our kynge and
there was greate bankettynge. And after
souper * there came in a maske mylady
marques of Penbroke † my lady Mary ‡
my lady Darby my lady Fitzwater my lady
Rocheford my lady Lislie and my lady
Wallop gorgyously apparayled with visers
on theyr faces and so came and toke the
frensshe kynge by the hande and other
lordes of Fraunce and daunced a daunce or
two. And after that the kynge toke of
theyr visers and than they daunced with
gentylmen of Fraunce an houre after. And
than they departed to theyr lodgynges.
And as for ye apparayle of ye frensshe
lordes my tongue can not expresse it and
in especyal the frensshe kyng his apparayle

---

* The Second Edition reads "soup" for "souper."
† Anne Boleyn.   ‡ Lady Mary Boleyn.

passed * my penne to wryte for he had a
dublet ouer set all with stones and ryche
diamondes whiche was valued by discrete
men at a hondred thousand pounde they
passed ferre our lordes and knyghtes in
apparayle and rychesse. They had greate
chere in Caleys and louynge also and all
at our kynges costes and charges. Also
the same daye that the kynges came from
Bulleyn the frensshe kynge made the duke
of Norffolke and the duke of Suffolke of
the ordre of saynt Mighill.† And vpon
monday whiche was the. xxix. day of
October at Caleys our kyng made the
great mayster of Fraunce and the admyrall
of Fraunce knyghtes of the garter. And
that daye there was a greate wrastelynge
betwene englysshe men and frensshe men
before bothe the kynges the frensshe
kynge had none but preestes that wrasteled
which were bygge men and stronge they
were bretherne but they had moost falles.‡

---

* The Second Edition reads "passeth" for "passed."
† Saint Michael.
‡ After "most falls" the Second Edition inserts,
"And as concernynge yͤ haboundaunt and lyberal mul-

And vpon the. **xxix.** daye of October the frensshe kynge departed fro Caleys to Parys ward and our kynge brought hym as ferre as Morgyson which is fro Caleys. vij. myle and so came to Caleys agayne. And he purposeth (god wyllynge) to be at Caunter- bury the. viij. daye of Nouember and so home whome god of his goodnes euer pre- serue and sende good passage and safe agayne into Englande. Amen.

God Saue the Kynge.

Imprynted by Wynkyn de Worde vnder tbe grace and preuylege of our moost royall and redoubted prynce Kynge henry tbe viii. for Johan Gowgb dwellinge at Poules gate in Cbepe.

Cum Priuilegio.

---

tytude of gyftes that were so louyngly and cordyally gyuen on bothe partyes (to the greate honour of bothe the kynges) my penne or capacit can not expresse it as well amonge the greate lordes as vnto the lowest yemen that bare ony offyce in eyther kynges hous and speci- ally the kynges gyftes on both partyes alway rewarded the one lyke vnto ye other And all other gyftes was nothynge but ryche plate golde coyne and syluer was of no estymacyon beside raymentes horses geldynges fawcons beres dogges for the game with many other whiche were to moche to write. And upon y^e **xxix.** day" &c.

The Noble

Tryumphaunt

Coronacyon of

Quene Anne.

The Noble Tryumphaunt Coronacyon of Quene Anne,

Wyfe unto the Moost Noble Kynge Henry the VIII.*

— —o— —

FIRST the. xxix. daye of Maye † beynge thursday all the worshypfull craftes ‡ and occupacyons in their best araye goodly besene toke theyr bargs which were splayed § wʰ goodly baners fresshe and newe with the cognysaunce and armes

---

* MS note : Q. Anne Bullen the second wife of K. Henry 8 was crowned at Westminster on Whitsonday the first of Iune Anno Domini MDXXXIII. This triumph is set forth at large in Stowes Chronicle.

† 1533.   ‡ City companies.   § Displayed.

of theyr faculty to the nombre of L. great barges comly besene and euery barge hauynge mynstrels makynge greate and sweete armony. Also there was the bachelers barge comly besene decked with innumerable baners and all about hangyd with ryche cloth of golde foystes * waytynge her upon decked † with a great shotte of ordynaunce whiche descended the ryuer afore all ye barges and the bachelers barge formest‡ and so folowynge in good araye and ordre euery crafte in theyr degree and ordre tyll they came to Greenwyche and there taryed abydynge the quenes grace which was a wonderfull goodly syght to beholde. Than at thre of the clocke the quenes grace cam to her barge and incontynent § all the cytezins with that goodly company set forth towards London in good arraye as before is sayd. And to wryte what nombre of gon shot what with chambres and great peces of ordynaunce

---

* Swift ships.   † Bedecked.   ‡ "Sic."
§ French, " *incontinent,*" immediately.

were shotte as she passed by in dyuers
places it passeth my memory to wryte or
to tell the nombre of them and specially
at Ratly and at lyme house out of certeyne
shyppes. And so ye quenes grace in her
ryche barge amonge her nobles the cytezyns
accompanyed her to London unto the toure
wharfe. Also or she came nere the toure
there was shot innumerable peces of
ordynaunce as euer was there by any
mennes remembraunces where the Kyng
receyued her grace with a noble louyng
countenaunce and so gaue great thankes
and prayse to all the cytezyns for theyr
great kyndnesse and louynge labour and
paynes in that behalfe taken to the greate
ioye and comforte of all the citezyns. Also
to beholde the wonderfull nombre of people
that euer was seen that stode on the shore
on bothe sydes of the ryuer was neuer in
one syght out of ye cyte of London sene
what in goodly lodgynges and houses that
be on ye ryuer syde bytwene Grenwyche
and London it passeth al mennes iudge-
mentes to esteme the infinyte nombre of

them. Wherein her grace with al her ladyes reioysed moche.

Knyghtes made at Grenwyche the sonday before Whytsonday.

And the sondaye before this tryumphe beyng the xxv daye of Maye the Kynge made at his maner of Grenwyche all these Knyghtes.

Syr Christofer Danby.
Syr Christofer Hylarde.
Syr Brian Hastynges.
Syr Thomas Methven.
Syr Thomas Butteller.
Syr Willyam Walgrave.
Syr Wyllyam Feldeyng.

The fryday made Knyghtes of the Bathe xix whose names foloweth.

Also on fryday the xxx day of Maye ye Kynge treated and made in the towre of London, xix. noble men Knyghtes of the bathe whose names folowe.

The lorde Marques Dorset.
The erle of Derby.
The lorde Clyfforde sone aud heyre to therle of Cumberlande.
The lorde Fitzwater sone and heyre to therle of Sussex.
The lorde Hastynges sone and heyre to therle of Huntyngton.
The Lorde Barkelay.
The lorde Mountagle.
The lorde Vaux.

Syr Henry Parker sone and heyre to ye lorde Morley.
Syr Wyllyam Wyndsour sone and heyre to the lorde Wyndesour.
Syr John Mordant sone and heyre to ye lorde Mordant.
Syr Fraunces Weston.
Syr Thomas Aroundell.
Syr Johan Hudelston.
Syr Thomas Ponynges.
Syr Henry Sauell.
Syr George Fitz Wyllyam of Lyncolne shire.
Syr Johan Tyndall.
Syr Thomas Jermey.

Also the saturday the last daye of May the Kynge made Knyghtes of the swerde in ye towre of London whose names folowe.

Syr Wyllyam Drury.	Syr Henry Feryngton.
Syr John Gernyngham.	Syr Marmaduc Tustall.
Syr Thomas Rusche.	Syr Thomas Halsall.
Syr Randolfe Buerton.	Syr Robert Thyrkham.
Syr George Caluerly.	Sir* Anthony Wyndsour.
Syr Edwarde Fytton.	Syr Water Hubbert.
Syr George Conyers.	Syr Johan Wyllongby.
Syr Robert Nedham.	Syr Thomas Thytson.
Syr Johan Chaworth.	Sir Thomas Mysseden.
Syr George Gresley.	Sir Thomas Fouleshurst.
Syr Johan Constable.	Sir Henry Delues.
Syr Thomas Umpton.	Sir Peter Warburton.
Syr John Horsley.	Sir Rycharde Bulkelley.
Syr Richarde Lygon.	Sir Thomas Lakyng.
Syr Johan Saintclere.	Sir Henry Lakyng.
Syr Edwarde Maidison.	Sir Water Smythe.

---

* Sic.

Sir Henry Eueringham.	Sir Johan Nories.
Sir Willyam Unedall.	Sir Willyam Malorie.
Sir Tho. Massyngberd.	Sir Johan Harcourt.
Sir Willyam Sandon.	Sir Johan Tyrell.
Sir James Baskeruille.	Sir Willyam Browne.
Sir Edmonde Trafforde.	Sir Nycolas Sturley.
Sir Arthur Eyre.	Sir Randolfe Manering.
Sir Henry Sutton.	

Also the sonday after Whytsonday beyng trynyte sonday and the viij. daye of
June was made at Grenewyche these
knyghtes followynge.

Sir Christofer Cowen.	Sir Johan Dawne.
Sir Geffray Mydelton.	Sir Richarde Haughton.
Sir Hugh Treuyneon.	Sir Thomas Langton.
Sir George West.	Sir Edwarde Bowton.
Sir Clement Herleston.	Sir Henry Capell.
Sir Humfrey Feryes.	

Also all the pauements of the cyte from
Charyncrosse to ye towre was ouer couerde
and caste with grauell. And the same
saturday beyng Whytson euen the mayre
with all the aldermen and the craftes of
the cyte prepared aray in a good order to
stande and receyue her and with rayles for
euery crafte to stande and leane from
prease of people. The mayre mette the
quenes grace at her comyng forthe of
ye towre and all his bretherne and alder-

men standyng in chepe. And upon the
same saturday the quene came forth from
ye towre towarde Westmynster in goodly
aray as here after foloweth. She passed
the stretes first with certayne straungers
then horses trapped w^h blewe sylke and
them selues in blewe veluet with white
fethers acompanyed two and two. Lyke-
wise squiers knights barons and baron-
etts knightes of ye bath clothed in vyolet
garmentes edged with armyns lyke iuges.
Than folowyng ye juges of the lawe
and abbottes. All these estats were to
ye nombre of CC. cople w^h more two
and two accompanyed. And than folowed
bysshops two and two : and tharch bysshops
of Yorke and Caterbury ye ambassaders of
Fraunce and Venyce the lorde mayre
w^h a mace mayster garter the kyng of
heraudes and the kings cote armour upon
him with ye offycers of armes apoyntyng
euery estate in their degre. Than folowed
two aunciente knights with olde fassion
hattes poudred on their heedes disgysed

who dyd represent ye duke of Normandy
and of Guyen after an olde custome : the
lorde constable of Englande for ye tyme
beyng ye duke of Suffolke the lorde
Willyam Hawarde ye deputie for ye tyme
to the lorde marshall duke of Norfolke.
Than folowed ye quenes grace in her
lytter costly and rychly besene w^h a ryche
canape ouer her which bare ye lordes
of ye fyue portes : after her folowyng
ye mayster of her horse w^h a whyte spare
palfray ledde in his hande rychly apoynted.
Than folowed her noble ladyes of estate
rychly clothed in crymosyn poudred
w^h armyns to the nobre of xij. Than
the mayster of ye garde with the garde on
both sydes of the strets in good aray and
all the constables well besene in veluet
and damaske cotes with whyte stanes in
their handes settynge euery man in araye
and orner in the stretes untyll she came
to Westminster. Than folowed four ryche
charyottes with ladyes of honour after
than folowed xxx. ladyes and gentylwomen

r(ich)ly * garnysshed and so y ͤ seruyng
men after them. And a(s) † she was departed from y ͤ towne a meruaylous great
shot of gonnes was there fyred and shot.
So this moste noble company passed till
her grace came to fanchurch where was
a pagent fayre and semly w ͪ certayne
chyldren which saluted her grace with
great honour and prayse after a goodly
fassyon : and so passed forthe to Grase
churche where was a ryght costly pagent
of Apollo with the nyne muses amonge
y ͤ mountaynes syttyng on y ͤ mount of
Pernasus and euery of them hauynge
theyr instrumentes and apparayle acordyng
to the descrypton of poets and namely of
Uirgyll with many goodly verses to her
great prayse and honour. And so she
passed forth through gracyous ‡ strete unto
leaden hall where was buylded a sumpt-

---

* In the originai copy, in the British Museum, the
corner is torn off after the letter "r" but the three
missing letters are of course "ich."

† The missing letter is as evidently "s."

‡ Gracechurch Street.

uous and a costly pagent in maner of a
castell wherein was fasshyoned an heuenly
roufe and under it vpon a grene was a
roote or a stocke whereout spronge a
multytude of whyte roses and reed
curyously wrought so from the heuenly
roufe descended a whyte faucon and lighted
upon ye said stocke and roote and incontynent descended an angell w^h goodly armony
hauynge a close crowne bytwene his
handes and set it on the faucons heed :
and on the said flour sate saynt Anne in
ye hyest place on that one syde her progeny w^h scripture that is to wete the thre
Marys w^h theyr issue y^t is to vnderstande :
Mary the mother of Christ Mary Solome
ye mother * of Zebedee with the two
chyldren of them also Mary Cleophe with
her husbande Alphee with their four
chyldren on ye other syde with other
poetycall verses sayd and songe w^h a balade
in englisshe to her great prayse (and) †
honour and to al her progeny also. And

---

* Wife.   † Torn away.

so she passed (for)th* from thence through
cornehill and at ye condyt was a sumptuous pagent of the thre graces : and at the
comynge of the quenes grace a poete
declared the nature of all those thre ladyes
and gave hye prayses vnto the quene. And
after his preamble fynysshed every lady
partyculer spake great honour and hye prayse
of the quenes grace : And so she passed
forth with all her nobles tyll she came
in chepe and at the great condyt was
made a costly fountayne whereout ranne
whyte wyne claret and reed great plenty
all that after noone : and ther was great
melody w^h speches. And so passed forthe
through chepe to the standarde whiche was
costly and sumptuously garnisshed with gold
and asure with armes and stories wher was
great armony and melody : and so passed
she forth by the crosse in chepe whiche
was newe garnisshed and so through chepe
towarde the lesser condyt. And in the
mydwaye bytwene the recorder of London

---

* Idem.

receyved her afore the Aldermen with
great reuerence and honour salutynge her
grace with a louyng and humble preposycion
presentynge her grace with a ryche and
costly purse of golde and in it a thousande
marke in golde coyne gyuen vnto her as a
free gyfte of honour : to whom she gaue
great thankes bothe with herte and mynde.
And so her grace passed a lytell further
and at the lesser condyt was a costly and a
ryche pagent where as was goodly armonye
ot musyke and other mynstrels with syngyng : And within that pagent was fyue
costly seates wherin was set these fyue
personages that is to wete Juno Pallas
Mercury and Venus and Parys hauyng a ball
of golde presentyng it to her grace with
certayne verses of great honour and chyldren
syngyng a balade to her grace and prayse to
all her ladyes and so passed forth to Poules
gate where was a proper and a sumptuous
pagent yᵗ is to wete ther sat. iij. fayre
ladyes virgyns costly arayde with a fayre
rounde trone ouer their heedes where

aboutc was written this. Regina Anna prospere procede et regna that is in cnglysshc Quene Anne prospere procede and reygne. The lady that sate in the myddes hauynge a table of golde in her hande wrytten with letters of asure. Ueni amica coronaberis. Come my loue . thou shallbe crowned. And two aungels hauyng a close crowne of golde bytwene their handes. And the lady on ye ryght hande had a table of syluer wherein was writte. Domine dirige gressos meos. Lorde god dyrecte my wayes. The other on the lyfte hande had in another table of syluer written thus. Confide in domino. Trust in god. And vnder theyr fete was a longe rol wherin was written this. Regina Anna nouum regis de sanguine natum cum paries populis aurea secla tuis. Quene Anne whan y^u shalte beare a newe sone of ye kynges bloode there shalbe a golden worlde vnto thy people. And so ye ladyes caste ouer her heede a multy-tude of wafers with rose leaues and about ye wafers were written with letters of gold this posay.* And so her grace passed forth into Poules chyrchyarde and at the eest ende of ye chyrch agaynst ye schole was a great scaffolde whereon stode ye nombre of two hundred chyldren well befene who receyued w^h poetes verses to her noble honour whan they had fynisshed she sayd Amen w^h ioyful smylyng countenaunce and so passed forth thrugh the longe chyrchyarde and so to Ludgate whiche was costly and sumptuously garnysshed with golde colours and asure with swete armony of ballades to her greate prayse and honour w^h dyuerse swete instrumentes. And thus her grace came thorowe the cyte with great honour and royaltye and passed thorowe Flete strete tyll she came to ye Standarde and condyth where was made a fayre toure with foure tourrettes with fanes there within great plenty of swete instrumentes w^h chyldren syngyng the

---

* The posy is not given in the original.

standarde of mason warke costly made
with ymages and aungels costly gylted
with golde and asure with other colours
and dyuerse fortes of armes costly set out
shall there contynue and remayne and
within the standarde a vyce with a chyme.
Also there ranne out of certayne small
pypes great plenty of wyne all that after-
noone. And so her grace passed through
the cyte to temple barre and so to Charyng
crosse and so thorowe Westmynster into
Westmynster hall where that was well and
rychly hanged with cloth of Arras with a
meruaylous ryche cupborde of plate and
there was a voyde * of spyce plates and
wyne. And y^t done the quenes grace
withdrewe her in to ye whyte hall for that
nyght and so to Yorke place by water.
The sondaye in ye mornynge at viij. of
the clocke ye quenes grace w^h noble ladyes
in theyr robes of estate w^h al ye nobles
aparayled in parlyament robes as dukes
erles archbysshops and bysshops w^h barons

---

* Collation.

and the barons of ye fyue portes * with the mayre of ye cite the aldermen in theyr robes as mantels of scarlet. The barons of ye fyve portes bare a ryche canopy of cloth of golde with stanes of golde and four belles of syluer and gylt. The abbot of Westmynster in his rygals † came in to ye hall in pontificalibus w^h his monkes in theyr best copes the Kynges chapell in theyr best copes with ye bysshops rychely aourned ‡ in pontificalibus and the ray cloth blewe spredde from the hygh desses of ye kynges benche unto the hygh aulter of Westmynster. And so every man procedynge to the mynster in ye best order euery man after theyr degree apoynted to theyr order and office as aperteyneth came vnto ye place apoynted where her grace receyued her crowne w^h al ye serymonyes therof as ther vnto belongeth. And so al

---

* Whenever the five ports are mentioned in the original a curious contraction is used at the end of the word probably for "es."

† Vestments.

‡ A misprint for adourned.

ye scrimonyes done w^h ye solempne masse they departed home in their best orders euery man to the hal of Westmynster where ye quenes grace withdrew her for a tyme in to her chambre apoynted and so after a certayne space her grace came in to ye hall. Than ye shulde haue sene euery noble man doyng their seruyce to them apoynted in ye best maner y^t hath ben sene in any suche scrimony. The quenes grace wasshed ye archbisshop of Canterbury sayd grace. Than ye nobles were set to the table therw^h came ye quenes seruice w^h ye seruyce of tharch bysshop a certayne space thre men with the quenes grace seruyce. Before ye said seruyce came ye duke of Suffolke high constable y^t day and stewarde of ye feest on horsbacke and meruaylously trapped in aparell w^h rychesse. Than w^h hym came ye lorde Wyllyam Hawarde as depute to ye duke of Norfolke in ye rome of ye marshal of Englande on horsbacke. The erle of essex caruer. Therle of Sussex sewer. Therle of Darby cupberer. Therle of Arundell butteller. The visconte lysle panter. The lorde Bray awmoner. These noble men dyd theyr seruyce in suche humble sorte and fassyon that it was wonder to se the payne and dylygence of them beynge suche noble personages. The seruyce borne by Knyghtes whiche were to me to longe to tell in order the goodly seruyce of kyndes of meate with their deuyses from the hyest vnto the lowest there haue not ben sene more goodlyer nor honorablyer done in no mannes dayes. There was foure tables in ye great hall alonge the sayde hall. The noble women one table syttyng al on ye one syde. The noble men an other table. The mayre of London an other table w^h his bretherne. The barons of the portes with ye mayster of the chauncery the fourth table. And thus all thynges nobly and tryumphantly done at her coronacyon her grace retourned to Whyte hall with great ioy and solempnyte and the morowe was great iustes at ye tylte done by xviij. lordes and knyghtes where was broken many speares valyauntly : but some of their horses wolde nat come at their pleasure nere unto the tylte whiche was displeasure to some that there dyd ronne.

Thus endeth this tryumphe: Imprinted at London in Fletestrete by Wynkyn de Worde for Johan Gougbe,

Cum Priuilegio.

www.ingramcontent.com/pod-product-compliance
Lightning Source LLC
Chambersburg PA
CBHW021436090426
42739CB00009B/1506